Richard Rohr, OF
of the New Mexico
ing Director of th
Contemplation in Albuquerque, New Mexico. An internationally recognized author
and spiritual leader, Fr. Richard teaches primarily on incarnational mysticism, non-dual
consciousness, and contemplation, with a
particular emphasis on how these affect the
social justice issues of our time. Along with
many recorded conferences, he is the author
of numerous books, including *Just This, What
Do We Do with the Bible?* and *The Universal
Christ: How a Forgotten Reality Can Change
Everything We See, Hope For, and Believe.* To
learn more about Fr. Richard Rohr and the
CAC, visit https://cac.org/richard-rohr
/richard-rohr-ofm/.

the world,
the flesh
and
the devil

RICHARD ROHR

the world,
the flesh
and
the devil

what do
we do
with evil?

Published in Great Britain in 2021

Society for Promoting Christian Knowledge
36 Causton Street
London SW1P 4ST
www.spck.org.uk

What Do We Do with Evil?
Copyright © 2019 Center for Action and Contemplation

Unless otherwise stated, Richard Rohr uses his own translation and/or
paraphrase of Scripture. Father Richard draws from a variety of English
translations including the Jerusalem Bible (JB), New American Standard
Bible (NASB), New English Translation (NET), J. B. Phillips
New Testament (Phillips), Revised Standard Version (RSV), and
The Message. CAC's practice is to reference chapter and verse
for scriptural sources, but not to identify precise translations.

British Library Cataloguing-in-Publication Data
A catalogue record for this book is available from the British Library

ISBN 978–0–281–08544–6
eBook ISBN 978–0–281–08549–1

1 3 5 7 9 10 8 6 4 2

Typeset by Nord Compo

Printed and bound in the UK by Jellyfish Print Solutions
eBook by Nord Compo

Produced on paper from sustainable forests

CONTENTS

INTRODUCTION

First we must fall, and then we recover from that fall—and both are the mercy of God.
—Julian of Norwich

I begin with this electrifying quote from Lady Julian of Norwich (1342–1416), my favorite woman mystic, who gives us so many liberating permissions, possibilities, and challenges, because I would like this thought to serve as the undercurrent for this book on the poorly understood concept of sin and the scary concept of evil. I hope you will soon see what I mean.

Let's start with sin. Doesn't it disturb you just a bit that the word "sin," which might just be the most common concept in the Bible, is so rarely used in many circles today? It is not that most of us want to deny the existence of evil and fault (which are more than obvious). Instead, for some reason, the word "sin" itself now seems old-fashioned and no longer helpful or even clarifying in most discussions. It can send any conversation down a rabbit hole of side comments, judgments, and clarifications that derail the original direction of the conversation. I see this across the board, with many progressives tending to hate the word and numerous conservatives tending to overuse it without defining it.

Perhaps so many of us stopped using the word because we located sin inside of our own small, cultural categories, with little awareness of the true subtlety, depth, and importance of the broader concept. As each culture and religion defined sin in its own idiosyncratic way, the word itself ceased being helpful. We Catholics, for example, eventually realized that eating meat on Friday had nothing to do with actual evil, but was simply contrary to a timebound church protocol and practice. Yet eating meat on Friday, along with not attending Mass on Sunday, have, since the sixteenth century, been called "mortal" sins (based on 1 John 5:16–17, which speaks of a "sin unto death"). Really? This realization led to mistrust of many things that supposedly "offended" God but largely just offended Christian Miss Manners.

We thus discovered that sin and true evil were not always the same thing. True evil is *always* deadly. Sin is meant to be a good and often-needed boundary marker, but it does not always point to objective evil and thus is not always deadly or "mortal." Even by our own Catholic definition, most sin was called "venial," which means pardonable, excusable, or easily forgivable.

Eventually, we realized there was no objective meaning to the word "sin." Instead, we simply used it to designate various taboos and cultural expectations, usually having

3

to do with bodily purity codes. Lay women wearing robes and headscarves was deemed virtuous in Islam but considered oppressive in most Christian countries. Working on the Sabbath was forbidden for Orthodox Jews, but it is probably the busiest day of the week for most families in the West. Some Catholics were into dancing and drinking, whereas many Southern Baptists would consider this almost obscene.

Are we pointing to anything like objective evil in such cases, or *are we actually trivializing the very real notion of evil and diverting our attention from the real thing?* Remember, the Third Reich emerged in a country that was formally half Catholic and half Lutheran—and seemingly quite serious about it, if we are to note all the churches and theological schools in Germany. So, who has the "right" or "real" definition of sin? Who has the "right" or helpful understanding of evil? I believe both Jesus and Paul do, and that will be the subject of this book.

4

My assumption and conviction are that sin became a less useful idea for many of us because *we needed to move around in a different field to regain our notion of the deadly nature of true evil.* No one can deny that evil is very real, but what many of us now observe as the real evils destroying the world seem very different from what most people call sin, which has mostly referred to personal faults or guilt, or supposed private offenses against God. These did not actually describe the horrible nature of evil very well at all. So, we lost interest in sin.

We also lost interest because we usually heard the concept of sin being used to judge, exclude, or control others, or to shame and control ourselves, but seldom to bring discernment or deeper understanding, much less compassion or forgiveness, to the human situation. In my observation, the more sin-obsessed a religion or culture became, the more unloving and cognitively rigid its people tended to be. Think of the shame-based

cultures of many homogeneous Islamic countries, the tribal and culturally uncritical forms
of Judaism, the humorlessness of Calvinist
Geneva, the cruelty of much of Puritan New
England, the graceless faith of many Luther-
ans, and the Inquisitional mindset of Spanish
and most ethnic Catholicism.

If we are honest and perceptive, we surely
see that actual evil often seems to "dominate
the very air" (a phrase found in Pauline texts
such as Ephesians 2:2) and is *more the norm
than the exception.* In fact, evil is often culturally agreed-upon, admired, and deemed necessary, as is normally the case when a country
goes to war, spends most of its budget on
armaments, admires luxuries over necessities,
entertains itself to death, or pollutes its own
common water and air. *Evil seems to be corporate, admired, and deemed necessary before it
becomes personal and shameable.* As the Apos-
tle Paul (or the school of Paul) wrote in the
condensed, tripart, and very instructive text
of Ephesians 2:1–2, "You were dead through

the crimes and sins that used to make up your way of life, when you were living by the principles of this world, thus obeying the ruler who dominates the very air."

Let's unpack this compact sentence, which seems to be pointing to at least three sources of evil: (1) "the crimes and sins that used to make up your way of life" (our personal participation in an already criminal and sinful culture), (2) "living by the principles of this world" (since most cultures are based on false or superficial agreements about value, dignity, and success), and (3) these illusions and deceits which so totally control the field of consciousness that most of us cannot see them. They "dominate" us, like the very air we breathe, and are never called into question. These sources will eventually be called the flesh, the world, and the devil, or the three classic sources of evil, which I will soon describe at length.

When some started to recognize (largely in the last century) that all the individual religious conversions in the world were not adding up to significant social change or moral advancement, many slowly began to realize that sin and evil must be more than personal or private matters. Convicting people of individual faults was not changing the world. Paul already had the prescient genius to recognize this, and I believe he taught that *both sin and salvation are, first of all, corporate and social realities.* In fact, this recognition could and should have been one of his major contributions to history. I believe it still will be.

Yet, we largely missed that essential point, and thus found ourselves in the tight grip of monstrous social evils in Christian nations, all the way down to the modern era. Thus we also lost out on the benefit of a corporate notion of salvation that far exceeded anyone's individual worthiness or unworthiness (which, sadly, became the whole Christian agenda and kept us small). I am convinced this was all described in Paul's letters, but with a pre-modern vocabulary that is no

longer easily accessible, as we see in the Ephesians quote above. But, once we do see it, we
will see it everywhere—either assumed or
actively taught in his letters. It is like breaking
his code.

I talked about the social notion of salvation in *The Universal Christ*.[1] Here, in a correl-
ative way, I would like to talk about the social
nature of evil and sin.

*We are all guilty with one another's sin and
not just our own.*

*We are all good with one another's goodness
and not just our own.*

My life is not just about "me."

If you can trust me on that, this will all
begin to make supreme sense. Only now do
we have the social tools, psychology, and
vocabulary to recognize this in a broad way.
Notions like group psychology, the genome
itself, family systems theory, codependency
studies, parenting styles, the unfreedom of
addiction (AA), the predictable behaviors of
adult children of addicts (Al-Anon), Girard's

mimetic theory, the broad evidence of neuroscience, the generational effects of trauma and war (PTSD), and the hidden nature of our personal shadow and most cultural agreements—all show that *the bandwidth of our actual personal freedom is much narrower than we once thought.* Yet, it can also be significantly expanded, which might just be the major goal of both psychology and healthy spirituality. In fact, I believe *this should be the result of good therapy and healthy spirituality: to expand our freedom to do good.*

We can no longer try to understand the individual apart from context, culture, religious belief, family, temperament, gender, DNA, birth order, and culture itself—which leads to the question of whether there can even be such a thing as a fully "self-made" person or a completely "authentic" individual. Sometimes it seems we are all on an ever-changing scale from rebels to conformists and some invisible voice is calling the shots. The "I" that is acting right now is never perfectly obvious, even to ourselves. My mother is still "making me do it" and I either (1) have been healed of any wounding, (2) learned to agree with her, or (3) am in perpetual and self-destructive war against her.

But here is some good news. If we are indeed objectively created in the "image and likeness" (Genesis 1:26–27) of a Trinitarian God, we are indeed, in our deepest essence, *relational*, so the relational self need not be considered a diminishment, but much more an enhancement and a freedom.[2] We literally are all in this human thing *together*! *We each carry our part of the universal weight of glory and the universal burden of collective sin.* Authentic spirituality always somehow repeats the head-touching-the-ground mantra of Native religion, which ends so many of its ceremonies with the phrase, "all our relations," with the emphasis on *all*—even the Divine. Atheists are not so much wrong or bad as just exclusionary of some of the relations that they often know nothing about. The agnostic or sociopath will often find himself or herself operating with "no relations": Jean-Paul Sartre's "Hell is—other people"[3] or Friedrich Nietzsche's self-made superman (*Übermensch*)[4] that stands alone and above.

With supreme irony, the modern/postmodern era has now made us excessively individualistic and almost obsessed with finding our distinctness, our specialness, our uniqueness. *The True Self "hidden with Christ in God" (Colossians 3:3) is all the profound, one-of-a-kind uniqueness we can ever handle*, but this deep and anchored self in the infinite Mind of God is altogether too well-hidden from postmodern, Western people.[5] All our eccentric hair styles, clothing, names, identities, and body piercings will never create the eternal True Self, but they often become another hidden conformity to passing standards that are almost always outside ourselves.

This makes it very hard to put Humpty Dumpty together again. The low self-esteem and even mental illness of so many people today leads me to think that the isolated individual is just too fragile to bear the common burden of sin and guilt—and too self-hating and self-doubting to carry the delight of their own divine image (which we once called the soul).

In this book, I would like to offer you some *widening* of our concept of sin and evil—and freedom too. Once we are free, we must logically be free to sin too. This message has been with us all the time, even in the Bible, but sin was largely seen as something to punish and exclude instead of something to *enlighten and educate* us. (In my opinion, this is the precise change Jesus made to his own tradition of retributive justice.)

Once we are told what sin and freedom might actually be, perhaps we can see when it is connected to actual evil and actual unfreedom, and when it isn't. Then, I hope we can see how helpful and even necessary the concept of sin is—and not just as a way to shame self or others, or to feel properly guilty before

13

God and others. Stay with me, and you might just agree. *I am not denying personal responsibility, but, in fact, offering some tools whereby we can be universally responsible and thus immensely increase our inner and outer freedom too.* (It is actually easier to be universally responsible than personally guilty, yet we wallow in personal guilt and shame.) Hold onto these notions for now.

Without some honest notion of sin, our moral compass has no North Star—and no South, East, or West. We will see that this much deeper meaning of evil is found in the largely social judgments of YHWH against the whole society, in the oracles of the prophets that were almost always aimed at Israel's *corporate evil. How did we not see that?* It is the relentless pattern. This approach is then fully assumed in the words and actions of Jesus and further explicitly taught in the letters of Paul.

I believe the main reason Jesus doesn't walk around convicting people (except hypocrites) of sin is that he knows people's evil first comes from a matrix, an agreed-upon delusion, a cultural lie. *People are more duped and intellectually lazy than they are malicious.* (Scott Peck said something like this years ago in his classic book *People of the Lie.*[6]) Our individualistic reading of the Scriptures and ourselves never allowed us to see this. We cannot find what we were not told or educated to seek.

It was natural for Paul to carry the socio-historical message because he was formed by a Jewish worldview, which was based on a covenant (a relationship of reciprocal love, caring, and loyalty) between YHWH and the collective, "the people of Israel," never really with the individual (Abraham, Noah, Moses, or David). In Jesus' and Paul's thinking, *sin and evil were first about the people as a whole, the cultural consensus, and not just personal behavior.* Jesus regularly damns the collective and hardly ever the individual: "Alas for you, Corazin! Alas for you, Bethsaida! . . . Capharnaum, you will be thrown down to hell!"

(Matthew 11:21, 23). We commonly read, "You Pharisees," but seldom, "You, Joe."

Both Jesus and Paul passed on to their disciples a collective and historical understanding of the nature of sin and evil, against which individuals still had to resist but in which they were usually totally complicit—just like today. The city, people, or nation were judged first, then the individual. This is no longer the starting point for many people, which is leaving us morally impotent. We do not reproach our towns, our own religion, or our nation, but Jesus did so regularly (see Matthew 11:20). Jesus laments over "Jerusalem, Jerusalem" more than once (Matthew 23:37), but we do not hear anything about Joe Blow in downtown Jerusalem, who is only convicted by his implied cooperation with the cultural mood of killing and stoning others. I think this is hugely important for our understanding of evil.

As a confessor, I know for a fact that many people beat their breasts about trivial

16

things—wasting their own time, God's time, and mine—while not spotting the real evils that are likely poisoning their hearts and minds and countries. I have often said that hearing most (not all!) Catholic confessions is like being stoned to death with marshmallows. We trained people to feel guilty about certain "sins" but allowed them to be almost blind and avoidant about the evils that are killing us all. Confessors, have you ever heard a confession of someone who convicts himself or herself of fouling the nest in which we are all living? I haven't. Nor have I once heard a confession concerning the tenth commandment. We inhabit an entire culture of coveting and consuming one another's possessions.

THE WORLD, THE FLESH,
AND THE DEVIL

Early Catholic moral theology taught that there were three major sources of evil: the world, the flesh, and the devil. My professor always added emphatically: "In that order!" Yet, up to now, most of us Christians have placed almost all of our attention on the second or "flesh" level. We have had almost no education in or recognition of what Paul meant by "the principles of the world" and even less on what he meant by "the ruler who dominates the very air." The world and the devil basically got off scot-free for most of Christian history. The implications have been massive, blinding, and hugely destructive, both for the individual and for society, leading to many twentieth-century catastrophes that often took place in Christian countries.

My hope is that this recognition of Paul's staggering insight will work to increase personal responsibility and human solidarity. Both sin and evil are much bigger categories than personal moral failure, which resulted from focusing almost entirely and even exclusively on the second-level sins of "the flesh."[7] The world and the devil have largely been able to avoid detection throughout much of Christian history. To use Ken Wilber's four-part description of the work of religion, most of us stayed at the first, "Cleaning Up" level of our personal behavior and never got to the more mature levels of "Growing Up," "Waking Up," or "Showing Up."[8]

Religion often considered its job to be policing sexuality and various "unclean" acts rather than addressing the more serious and pervasive forms of corporate injustice and evil. Did it ever strike you as strange that a girl or young woman's participation in all of the early stage sacraments (baptism, first communion, often confirmation, and marriage) *demanded* that she wear white? Boys, on the other hand, started "pure" by wearing white at baptism, but then wore dark slacks or suits afterward. So, even Cleaning Up was not equally applied, and had racist overtones besides.

Evil is subtle and the evils that are killing us all are usually well-disguised (which is exactly why they *are* killing us!). Thomas Aquinas (1225–1274) taught that humans *usually do evil by choosing an apparent good,* which means a good from the perspective of the small and unconverted ego. *Most people who do evil have fully explained it to themselves as good* (meaning it is good for them), regardless of whether it is objectively good or good for society as a whole. Injustice, for example, always profits *somebody.* Justice is usually denied to a minority of some kind. All a politician has to do is put such a spin on it and people will often vote against their own legitimate self-interest to follow the demagogue or the group. Some theorists have called such voters "useful idiots."

This is exactly and primarily why evil gains such ascendency in this world. "Good people" do very bad things, symbolized by "when they kill [Christ and] think they are doing a holy duty for God" (John 16:2). The only quote I have on my hermitage wall from my father St. Francis of Assisi (1182–1226) is this: "We must bear patiently *not* being good . . . and not being *thought good.*"[9] Yes, he said that! It is recorded in his oldest biography. For centuries, we Franciscans thought it was a typo because it was so counterintuitive. It is dangerous to need to think of ourselves as good, or to need others to think we are clean, pure, and above reproach. It leads us all to become hypocrites. This is the ego speaking, which does not really care about objective goodness, for itself or others. It just wants to *look good* in the eyes of society and in its own self-image.

Thus, Jesus recommends that prayer, almsgiving, and fasting all be done "in secret"

(Matthew 6:1–18). We, however, *want* everybody's left hand to know exactly what our right hand is doing—when it is doing good, that is (Matthew 6:3). We must humbly admit that, for most of us, looking good is more important than simply and quietly being good—and we must go further. Conformity with the loudest group's mood is—for many people, maybe even for most people—equated with being moral. Remember, the public mood is another way to describe "the world," evil's first hiding place—to *appear to be,* more than to actually *be.* Real saints are seldom simple conformists; they go wherever Love leads them, even if and when it makes them appear not to be loving. Jesus himself is a good example.

PAUL'S SPIRITUAL GENIUS

These are the only genuine ideas; the ideas of the shipwrecked. All the rest is rhetoric, posturing, farce.

—José Ortega y Gasset

Isn't it ironic and interesting that Paul was literally shipwrecked three times (2 Corinthians 11:25)? And isn't it more than interesting that the Twelve Step Program makes the first step on the journey to recovery the experience of *absolute powerlessness*? Apparently, there is something spiritually essential that we do not know until we hit rock bottom or face life's injustice and absurdity in a quite personal way. Life is not fair at all!

This is one of Paul's great ideas. For him, sin is not primarily individual fault, but the negative matrix out of which both evil and enlightenment arise ("the world"), which then often leads to the glorification of "my" evil as good and necessary for society ("the devil"). This makes good people do bad things and bad people do very bad things—without a whiff of guilt or shame (conscience cannot yet be formed at this level because the ego is still steering the ship). It usually takes a "shipwreck" of some kind to begin the formation of a truly mature conscience. Before that, we just focus on religious and social protocols.

This appears to be Paul's summary teaching about sin and evil:

- "The world" is advantageous, denied, and disguised evil.
- "The devil" is sanctified, glorified, and romanticized evil. ("The angels of darkness must disguise themselves as angels of light" [2 Corinthians 11:14].)

26

• "The flesh" imitatively buys into both these ideas. (The mimetic theory of René Girard [1923–2015] is very helpful here. Basically, he says we are all copycats, both of good and of evil. We just need models for both and we easily mimic their behavior.[10])

Most of the rest of this book will illustrate how this is true. Because it is so subtle, I describe it below from many angles. I will ground it all with this astounding statement from Paul: *"For it was to vanity that creation was subjected. Not because of any fault of its own is it unable to attain its full purpose, but it was made so by God"* (Romans 8:20). God seems to have created a deliberately incomplete and imperfect universe, so we could be in on making it whole and holy. Evil is the fly in the ointment that sets the whole drama in motion. There has to be a "villain" for us to work against. This is probably the summary sentence expressing Paul's universal cosmology of evil.

Evil is our inability to ever be perfect, pure, and deathless, but Paul follows this pronouncement with an exit strategy, throwing us a life preserver: "Creation still retains a hope of being freed from its enslavement to corruption, to enjoy the same freedom and glory as the children of God" (Romans 8:21). Nature and human nature follow the same universal pattern: Life > Death > Life. Order must be confronted with disorder to find its full self (reorder). There is no stopping at some ideal order, nor is there a nonstop flight to reorder. Paul will call this "the folly of the cross" in several places (1 Corinthians 1:18, for example). Liberals don't like any assertion of order. Conservatives will not tolerate disorder. They are both half-blind.

Paul is teaching that *sin is a word for the basic absurdity of life* on this earth, the impossible situation, the tragic sense of life that we all eventually face, perhaps best summed up in the realization that, "You can never win" or "Vanity of vanities, all is vanity"

28

(Ecclesiastes 1:2). Somehow, *failure is always part of the deal.* Everything passes away, and—worse—we see that we ourselves are much of the problem, despite our best efforts to the contrary. We are trapped in a dilemma that we cannot *fully* resolve or overcome. (Until we know this, we are not ready for God's unique uplift!)

Paul seems to think that sin is fully allowed to dwell within us and in our world: "Jews and Greeks [the two major symbolic groups] are all under sin's dominion" (Romans 3:9); "Both Jews and Greeks have sinned and forfeited God's glory" (Romans 3:23); "Death's dominion has spread through the whole human race" (Romans 5:12). Paul believes failure and fault have an inevitability to them, from which no one can escape, despite both religion/law ("the Jews") and reason/philosophy ("the Greeks").

Here are some of those angles for approaching Paul's thought:

• "Creation had frustration imposed upon it, but for divine purposes" (my translation of Romans 8:20). The way forward is not a straight line and never will be. This is not the Western philosophy of progress. Evolution and growth are not on a straight line and never have been.

• Our entrapment in this "law of sin and death" (Romans 8:2) reveals *the core absurdity of the human situation.* The tragic nature of all life is that it must include death in some form. Paul thus preceded the modern existentialists and postmodern cynics by many centuries. He was able to effectively (even triumphantly) include disorder inside of order, which few besides Jesus have done. Most insist on purity codes and debt codes, exclusion or punishment of fault, instead of *using disorder and including sin and death in the very solution.* As the Benedictus (prayer of Zechariah) puts it, "You will be given the knowledge of salvation through the forgiveness of sins" (Luke 1:77). *Note the prayer does not say we will have knowledge of salvation through the perfect avoidance of sin, but precisely through the transformative power of forgiveness of sin*—which he calls, in the next line, "the tender mercies of our God" (1:78).

♦ While insisting in all his letters on the human person as the living image of God (see 1 Corinthians 3:16–17; Romans 5:5), thus giving us a very positive anthropology, Paul wrote, "It is not my true self that does bad things, but sin that lives within me" (Romans 7:17, 20). *We are all a living conflict.* "Who will deliver me from this body of death?" he finally sighs in anguish (Romans 7:24). He is not referring to his personal physical body here, but this "law of sin and death" (8:2), which seems inevitable and ubiquitous. It is much more a *universal negative force field* than some kind of blotch inside of people (which usually became "*some* people, but not me"). The only *permanent stamp* in us is the indwelling Holy Spirit (8:9–11), which he variously calls the pledge, the promise, and the guarantee—but there is

31

a fly in the ointment. Such a warranty, being participation in the very life of God, includes and transcends any negative charge.

• Paul wrote, "Human nature, left to itself, is opposed to God, does not submit to God's law, and *indeed it cannot*" (Romans 8:7). Wow! Talk about futility. We are "bodies of clay who are carrying a great treasure" (2 Corinthians 4:7). We are given a thorn in the flesh to keep us from getting too proud, an angel of Satan to buffet us (2 Corinthians 12:7). Paul uses these metaphors to explain the source of this seemingly inherent sin. "I do not understand my own actions, for I do not do what I want, but I do the very thing I hate" (Romans 7:15). He was clearly not an evil person, yet, in a moment of self-disgust, he wrote, "I have been sold as a slave to sin" (Romans 7:14). The whole context reveals, not a kind of personal guilt or shame, but a social entrapment, a shared dilemma, an imprisonment in a mixed and impure reality. Even moral commandments only remind him

32

of this: "I should not have even known what it means to covet if the law had not said, 'You shall not covet'" (Romans 7:7). Maybe this irony is the source of many people's resentment and denial of moral commandments today. Such mandates often serve to drive our helplessness and hopelessness deeper, as we know that we cannot carry out most of God's serious commandments (love your enemies, give your money to the poor), but only the easy ones that can be measured externally (go to church on Sunday).

◆ Sin is *the seeming final victory of death*, which always has the last word on everything (Romans 5:12–7:25). Nothing lasts forever, or even for very long, despite our best attempts at personal "immortality projects," as Ernest Becker calls them.[11] Everything passes or finally disappoints us and invariably shows us its weakness. As Eckhart Tolle said after the 9/11 disaster, "Even the sun will die."[12]

◆ Note how frequently Paul uses the unusual concept of "the law of sin" or the "law

33

of sin and death," which I call *the sin system.* There is not much point in thinking we live outside of it or are above it. It is a systemic problem, a web that catches us all in different ways. To think we are above it becomes the one sin of hypocrisy that Jesus so vehemently criticizes (Matthew 23) or maybe even "the sin against the Holy Spirit" (Matthew 12:31) that he says cannot be forgiven—precisely because such illusion does not think it needs forgiveness. Most of us are basically nice people—inside of very narrow explanations, petty reward/punishment frames that we then pass on to our children, who then begin the denial-and-scapegoating process all over again. Was this the universal entrapment that Augustine first called "original sin"? I personally think so. We are all in the sin system together, and we all pass on some of it through the woundedness that we cannot see in ourselves, but only in others, which is surely why we *must* love our chosen enemies (because there our shadow is trying to reveal itself to us).

• Evil is, first of all, fully agreed upon as good and necessary—a reality to which we are all blind or we deny. I call it *group narcissism* because it is in the crowd that evil most effectively hides. This is true of all the seven deadly sins: pride, envy, avarice, lust, sloth, gluttony, and wrath. Think about it, and you will see that each of these also has a positive face.[13] *Evil is usually deemed good before it shows itself as also bad.* This can be seen in almost every violent revolution in the history of the world and almost all attempts at reform of anything. Turning over these rocks and seeing the other side, where evil festers, is now called "shadow work" or, for some of us, Enneagram work.

• *To think we can totally resist and avoid all evil is to persist in it in a new form.* Every action is met by an equal and opposite reaction, as the laws of physics state. So, we must find a response to evil that is other than mere reaction or resistance. Ironically, that new response will first look like acceptance—but it develops and envelops much more than that. This will always be utterly counterintuitive to most humans. Most of us cannot tolerate what clearly looks like disorder or "the folly of the cross" (1 Corinthians 1:18). If the postmodern nihilist believes "nothing means nothing," then the Gospel of Jesus and Paul is saying *even nothing means something*! But I am jumping ahead.

• Paul recognized our inability to ever be totally perfect and above criticism, despite observance of the laws and rituals of religion (Romans 7:1–13; Galatians 3:1–29). He saw where preoccupation with the law had led him and his fellow Pharisees (Philippians 3:6–7): It made him self-righteous and even violent. Thus, he shamelessly wrote, "Cursed be the law" if we rely on it instead of on loving faith (Galatians 3:10). His code word for any group that trusts too much in law and ritual is "the Jews," not as a specific religion, but as an archetype of all religions in their Cleaning Up and tribal stages. He names himself as one of these, and fervently so

(Philippians 3:5–6), but he recognizes that this very fervor led him to extreme and self-justified violence.

• We cannot find validation or liberation inside of either religion or cultural boundaries when they are closed and finite systems, because it only works for those who agree with that same system! This is what leads Paul to his *critique* of the ethnic Judaism in which he was raised. Yet, he also expresses his utter *gratitude for it* because Judaism sent him into this necessary conflict and ultimately onto the right path (Romans 9–11). Many of us would say the same of the Christian churches today—but note the non-dual thinking!

• On the other side, there is no way for educated and thinking people to ever have a logical or satisfying answer to the problem of evil and death, so they tend to become cynics and unbelievers in some form. Paul's code word for those who trust in reason and education is "the Greeks," or sometimes "the philosophers." He asked, "Where are the philosophers now? Where are any of our thinkers today? . . . Has not God made foolish the wisdom of the world? For Jews demand signs and Greeks desire wisdom, but we proclaim Christ crucified, a stumbling block to the Jews and foolishness to the Gentiles. . . . For God's foolishness is wiser than human wisdom" (1 Corinthians 1:20–25). Instead of embracing law and knowledge as saviors, Paul makes a preemptive leap into *the safety of Divine vulnerability, the powerlessness of nonviolence, and the shame of identification with the losers—where the ego cannot hide.* He believes this is the marrow of the Gospel that Jesus lived out in his lifetime. "When I am weak, I am strong" (2 Corinthians 12:10) seems to be his motto. This is contrary to the rules and expectations of almost every culture in the world, which is why the Gospel is emerging so slowly in history.

• Thus, both virtue and sin are ambiguous. *To some real degree, we must "suffer" and "hold" both with caution.* Virtue is, in fact, usually a choice for a partial good (that almost always has some bad effects for oneself or others; see Romans 7:14–25), as evidenced in the Pharisaical temptation to perfection and judgment found in almost all high-minded or religious groups. Almost every new governmental law or policy is partially good for some and not so good for others. Paul also recognizes that sin itself is often a choice for evil which, though tragic and hard to admit, can also have some good effects for oneself or others! (The crucifixion itself is our prime, mind-blowing example.) Both sin and virtue are themselves caught in this non-dual matrix where good and bad exist simultaneously, much like the weeds and the wheat, which Jesus tells us should be allowed to "grow together until the harvest" (Matthew 13:30).

   • We might fear that such thinking would lead to moral relativism, and *it will indeed with willful, ignorant, and opportunistic people.* Both the weakness and the genius of "the freedom of the children of God" (Galatians 5:13–25) is that God risks everything for the sake of love, which can only emerge in freedom, not under duty or duress. God trusts freedom so far as to fully allow us to sin. It's pretty obvious, isn't it?

• But, in people of good will, the effect of this realization about sin and freedom is quite often true compassion, an empathetic sadness, and a quiet gift of patience and humility. Its greatest effect is love of God and of neighbor—a love that never stops deepening. Mistakes themselves become another occasion to experience the "generosity of mercy" and the "infinite richness of grace" (Ephesians 2:4–10), instead of just an excuse to hate ourselves.

• In Paul's way of thinking, humans are inherently unstable, grabbing for legitimation which they never totally find. He believes that the only way through this reality is by surrender to an infinite Source of validation, which gives us the one and only reliable ground (Romans 8:38–39; 1 Corinthians 13:1–13). All else is posturing and pretending, he believes. I know that sounds like a stock religious answer, but after forty-nine years of religious counseling and spiritual direction, it seems to me to be absolutely true.

- Perhaps Paul's greatest realization about the nature of sin and evil is that evil is given a pass because we all need it too much and it is so perfectly disguised (the "spirits in the air" in Ephesians 2:2, or the frequently alluded-to powers, principalities, thrones, and dominations). We cannot fully localize it by name or in one person, country, religion, or institution, even though we all try to find concrete villains or scapegoats to blame for our problems. Radical egocentricity ("I" as the reference point) is all around us, taken for granted, taken for good, and well-nigh invisible—until it is exposed by its inability to love and to suffer for those we love.

In summary, Paul would probably say:

- *The individual is not so much the isolated initiator of evil as the actual victim of it.*

41

  • The point of the Gospel is to keep people from buying into the "sin systems" and to retain their freedom.

  • Don't become a victim. Find your freedom by transferring your love and loyalty to another positive and non-reactive Center, which is Christ!

I will now take up some of Paul's insights in greater depth so that we may fully appreciate and understand the ways in which sin and evil operate in our lives.

WE ARE ALL PROFITING FROM
AND COMPLICIT IN EVIL

The stagnation of my prayer life . . . is due to deep involvement in the collective sin of American society and American Catholicism—a sin of which we all refuse to be aware. How offer to God prayer as an act of justice when I am living in injustice? An injustice which pervades the whole world and is even greater in the camp of those who can see that we are exploiters. They are worse.

—Thomas Merton

Our narrow notion of sin as primarily personal has left both history and the church quite naïve about the true nature of evil and thus highly subject to it, at both the highest and lowest levels of most Christian cultures. In the quote from Ephesians 2:1–2, note that all three sources of evil are together named as almost overlapping—and they are all described as states of "deadness," by which I think Paul means states of unconsciousness. In contrast, we think of states of moral impurity, in which Jesus showed no interest.

When we love authentically, we are always highly conscious. When we deliberately do evil, we have to be unconscious. To repeat, Paul teaches throughout that we are unconscious (dead) through at least three sources: personal sins, the agreed-upon customs of this world, and the "ruler who dominates the very air." Since the deadness proceeds from at least three sources, this makes it very hard to place blame precisely and appropriately (which is why we all long to scapegoat; it takes away our anxiety when we think we have localized evil). Law cannot fully locate it (witness our unhappiness with so many legal verdicts), nor can the individualized conscience,

44

nor can some perfect social analysis—there is always another cause too. "Sin is master everywhere," Paul wrote in Galatians (3:22).

For me, this is exactly why both Jesus and Paul are so aware of the danger and limitations of law, by itself, to solve the human problem. "If you pass judgment, you have no excuse, it is yourself that you are condemning" (Romans 2:1). Why did he write this? Because rash judgments are our very problem—if they end up making us aloof, separate, or superior. Maybe we can start with such dualistic clarity, but we must not stay there. Our responses must eventually morph into compassion and forgiveness toward the offender. This is the "power from on high" for the "forgiveness of sins" (Luke 24:47–49) instead of the usual counting of offenses. We are now in a different economy of grace and mercy that allows us to let go, trust, and love instead of paying back in kind. This is the reward of the Gospel.

Because no law can ever address all three levels, it will always be imperfect and inadequate to the task. So, Paul actually wrote, "Cursed be the law," in Galatians 3:10, which is certainly not what we expect to hear from a religious teacher. Jesus himself says, in effect, and six times in a row, "the law says, but I say" in Matthew 5:21–45. They both seem to think that while *law can name the problem, it cannot really resolve it in any fundamental way.* (Go, sue someone in court and see if it really makes you happy or changes the actual situation.) The seven deadly sins are still at work. It is really astounding that the Christian religion created so many "law and order" people, given this radical critique of law by the two major sources of New Testament teaching.

In addition, laws primarily protect the powerful, seldom the powerless. Our bias was so strongly toward the top that it took us a long time to see this, perhaps only beginning with the French Revolution of 1789 (even if it did so in a very violent way). I cannot help but think of Robert Bolt's play, *A Man for All Seasons.* Its main character, Thomas More, the sixteenth-century Chancellor of England, refused to endorse King Henry VIII's wish to divorce his first wife. In the play, More describes Christians as "hiding in the thickets of the law" and being "anchored to [their] principles,"[14] often to avoid the true purpose of the law. It is almost the norm for those in power to use the law to support what they want to do—or excuse what they have already done. Expedience and ambition will always find a law or a scripture to justify their power grab.

THE HIDING PLACES
OF DEADNESS

I will now briefly describe how the world, the flesh, and the devil each serve as different hiding places for *deadness* or *unconsciousness*, so that you will be able to see them for yourself. It seems evil must be quite correctly named in order to be seen and exorcised (see Mark 5:8–9). Both Thomas Aquinas in his *Commentary on the First Epistle to the Corinthians* and C. S. Lewis (1898–1963) in *The Screwtape Letters* taught that the triumph of evil entirely depends on disguise. Our egos must see it as some form of goodness and virtue (and a benefit to us) so that we can buy into it. So, any advantage or disadvantage to *me* is never the real issue on which goodness or evil depends!

49

Yet, that is where we all begin and why *the movement beyond oneself as the reference point is the only real foundation for any spiritual journey.*

Kings and politicians know well that by promising people personal security or prosperity for themselves or their group, they can lead those people almost anywhere. Fear and security are, of course, the lowest levels of human motivation. These are not bad motives, but they are not the motives that create a large and equitable society. They only create warring tribes. How do we get people to climb up to some kind of higher motive, like freedom for all and love for all? That should be the pressing concern of any religion or society worthy of the name.

THE WORLD

If evil depends on a good disguise, the cover of cultural virtue and religion is the very best of all. Remember the full conspiracy (see Luke 23:12) between the Roman Empire's representative (Pilate) and the Jewish High Priest (Caiaphas) in the killing of Jesus? Through this conspiracy, Christians were forewarned that even the highest levels of power (Rome and Jerusalem) can and probably will be co-opted by evil—and most will not see it, precisely because of this common entrapment in personal importance, our idolization of power, and inflated self-images— what John calls "the sensual body, the lustful eye, and the pride of life" (1 John 2:16).

Is there a culture in this world that does not operate out of this recipe for delusion? No wonder history books are largely the history of wars. This is what Paul means when he names "the world," or what I call the system, as one of the sources of evil, maybe even the matrix. What he already recognized, at least intuitively, is that *it is almost impossible for any social group to be corporately or consistently selfless.* It has to maintain and promote itself first.

51

(If you don't want to hear that, it might reveal the depth of the disguise of institutionalized evil.)

The Desert Fathers and Mothers of the fourth century tried to escape this lie entirely, the Franciscans tried for a time to offer an alternative society, and others have also sought to counter the powers of the world. But only a few groups, like the Amish, the Bruderhof, the Catholic Worker movement, Tibetan Buddhism, some monasteries, and a few other groups have succeeded in some measure. To do so, they always needed to enforce total conformity and homogeneity, which only works for a few and for a short time. Individuation, freedom, human maturity, and personal conscience were invariably diminished or lost.

I remember my own novice master reminding us young friars in 1961 (a time of intense fear of communism) that we had joined a communal and shared organization and we were now, in fact, "communists!" After we got over our initial shock—he let us sit in silence for a few minutes—he said, "But ours is a free and chosen poverty, whereas Marxist communism is enforced and conformist poverty—and that makes all the difference."

Lest we think the corporate and hidden character of sin and evil is a distant or theoretical issue, we must ask how the seemingly sincere Catholic Church was able to produce, deny, and cover up its pedophilia crisis for decades (centuries?) despite two thousand years of moral teaching and formation. Furthermore, how does the well-ordered United States government, with three rational levels of checks and balances and "one person, one vote," still produce the broad political dysfunction, foundational immorality, and gross deceit from which America suffers today? How does as much as 40 percent of the US population see no real problem with this state of affairs? After all our religion, higher education, reformations, and revolutions, it seems we are still quite capable of full complicity in the deeds of death. Religions, governments, and all corporations and organizations are highly capable of evil while not recognizing it as such—because it profits *us* for them to be immoral. Evil finds its almost perfect camouflage in the silent agreements of the group when it appears personally advantageous.

Such deadness will continue to show itself in every age, I believe. This is what the multifaceted word "sin" is still trying to reveal. If we do not see the true shape of evil or recognize how we are fully complicit in it, it will fully control us, while not looking the least like sin. Would "agreed-upon delusion" be a better description? We cannot recognize it or overcome it as isolated individuals, mostly because it is held together by the group consensus. We need to be in solidarity with alternative communities and minority groups to see it. The dominant group normally cannot see its lies—in any country or context. It is the air we are breathing, reaffirmed at every cocktail party of like-minded people. We have

54

to pay attention to whoever is saying, "I cannot breathe" to recognize the biases at work.

Evil is all around us, in common agreements that we take for granted, like America's and Canada's full involvement in the "necessary" breaking of almost every treaty we signed with the Native peoples of North America. I am not attempting to justify such injustices and dishonesty, but I am afraid it will always be this way. Rather than seeing this stark reality in a defeatist or fatalistic way, we can actually recognize it as also empowering. When we do not expect perfect and total victory (which nobody ever gets anyway), we are much more able to stay committed to efforts for incremental changes and improvements. Righteous and absolutist moral victories (like the US Prohibition law banning alcohol in the 1930s and the attempts to build walls in Berlin, Israel, or on the US-Mexico border) only produce temporary and eventually disastrous results.

The beginning of a way out is to *honestly see what we are doing.* The price we will pay is that we will no longer fit in the dominant group! Mature religion must train us to recognize the many camouflages of evil, or everyone's future will always be dominated by some form of denied deadness, and not just for the oppressed group; the oppressor dies too, just in much more subtle ways.

God is clearly a Great Allower and seldom controls the show in this world. Jesus even goes so far as to say that "Satan is the prince of this world" (John 14:30), but he is already *exposed and thereby condemned* (John 16:11)—once we recognize the games of the world. The "kingdom" that Jesus talks about is what the world would be like if God actually did control the show. It is always "coming" and never fully here, as we pray for so constantly in the Lord's Prayer. This is why some form of faith or trust is necessary.

THE FLESH

The second source emerges from the first and creates victims. Paul usually uses the word "flesh" as a negative term for anything purely human, individual, passing, partial, and thus tricky and untrustworthy. This shows itself in our private crimes and sins. But these are the effects and corollaries (rather than the causes) of our previously agreed-upon way of life (named in the Ephesians 2:1–2 quote) which is fully legitimated by "the principles of this world." *Personal sin is not the primary cause of malice as much as it is the result of a deeper lie or illusion.* Personal evil is committed rather freely because it is derived from and legitimated by our underlying, unspoken agreement that certain evils are necessary for the common good.

However, if we would be honest, this leaves us very conflicted. War is good and necessary, but murder is bad. National or corporate pride is good, but personal vanity is bad. Capitalism is good, but personal gluttony or greed is bad (or, at least, it used to be). Lying and cover-ups are good to protect the whole (the church, American self-interest, governments), but individuals should not tell lies. This is our foundational confusion and moral schizophrenia. We cannot put all our focus on changing the world at the individual, "flesh" level. Individual changes never really accumulate into significant cultural or social change, but that is where we have put almost all our attention up to now, with very limited success.

THE DEVIL

Now we come to the most sophisticated revelation, at this third level. The spiral of violence has been increasing and is now a full Category 5 tornado. Remember, when Paul seemingly

talks about the devil, he is not really referring to winged creatures or red demons with
pitchforks. He uses words like "powers,"
"principalities," "spirits in the air," "sover-
eignties," "thrones," and "dominations." They
are almost certainly his premodern words for
what we would now call corporations, institutions, nation states, and organizations that
demand our full allegiance and thus become,
in many ways, idolatrous—not just "too big
to fail," but even too big to be criticized. Sud-
denly, the medieval notion of devils becomes
very close to home and very hard to deny. Yet
we have succeeded in our denial in almost
every culture and century, which is why evil
flourishes everywhere, especially in the form
of injustice.

If "the world" is denied and disguised evil
in corporate form, and it remains in control,
it soon becomes "spirits in the air" that do
immense damage but are invisible and unaccountable. "The devil," therefore, is *those same
corporate evils when they have risen to sanctified,*

romanticized, and idealized necessities that are saluted, glorified, and celebrated in paychecks, retirement accounts, parades, songs, rewards for loyalty, medals, and monuments. Who can question these? That's how disguised the "devil" is! We all join in on bended knee. If we refuse to bend the knee to the proper idol, we will be publicly mocked by the Establishment—and, in the US, by the president himself.

We must first convict religion in its organizational form—not its adherents, who might be quite good and holy, but the glorified organization itself. Then we must consider nation states, war economies, penal systems, police states, the banking system, the healthcare system, the pharmaceutical system, education systems, etc. They are all good and necessary, in and of themselves, but unless they are constantly held to public account and transparency—I am going to dare to say the unsayable—*they usually become demonic in some form,* and we normally cannot see it until it is too late.

60

Paul knew these forces that were really running the show were *hidden inside of common agreements that every culture idealizes for its own survival.* I think this is also what he was referring to when he (and his school) wrote of the "elemental principles of this world" (Colossians 2:8, 20; Galatians 4:3, 9) and "groveling to angels" (Colossians 2:18). These are the dark spirits that cannot be properly named, controlled, or contained because they have become invisible to us and even look like good angels. They seem to vanish into the air or to be entirely diffuse so that we all feel powerless to address them and require divine assistance (Romans 8:38–39; Ephesians 1:20–21, 3:10, 6:12; Galatians 4:3–5; Colossians 2:15, 20). Whom do you hold accountable for the huge rate of white-collar crime? How do you punish a system of thought like nationalism, or address the price of medicines in the US? How do you expose the polluting sources of the toxic air that all must breathe?

This is why most of us feel powerless at this third level. We just don't know where the negativity is localized. We try the court system to find remedies, but massive injustice, sexual harassment, and racial bias just morph into new forms. The demon is still out there. Its names are still gluttony, greed, pride, wrath, and avarice, but those sound so old-fashioned and judgmental. This is surely why the devil was almost always described as a shapeshifter or a trickster. Such evil remains fully in charge and in control, beyond the boundaries of any one individual. We know we are inside of the power of such "spirits" whenever we feel helpless, powerless, inept, enraged, and literally *dispirited* at a meeting, in our families, or at our jobs. At that moment, we are indeed "possessed" by a demon.

Because most of us lack any real understanding of sin (often limiting it to sex and alcohol—and maybe not even those anymore), Satan can easily operate as "the prince of this world," as Jesus says three times in

John's Gospel (12:31, 14:30, and 16:11) and the "ruler who dominates the very air," as we find in Ephesians (2:2). Only in our time have terms for this demonic evil emerged, such as "the military-industrial complex," the infallible "laws of the market," or "the white male system" (as Anne Wilson Schaef called it[15]). The title of Schaef's first book names our dilemma well: *When Society Becomes an Addict.*

If a term has an *-ism* at the end, it is usually an addictive potion and highly open to the demonic. It will always be *used by people seeking power without love* (communism, rigid capitalism, fascism, racism, consumerism, righteous feminism, heady liberalism, on and on). Pretty much anything society actually needs (security, healthcare, jails, banks, education) is highly subject to demonic usage.

These demonic powers are indeed flying around unnoticed, fully in control, just as premodern people thought of them—as "armies of angels" (albeit bad angels!). For centuries, we called the tyrant "who fell from the heavens" (Isaiah 14:12) Lucifer, which means *light-bearer.* This is still a common name for the devil. Most evil carries a seductive kind of small light for a few, as with white supremacists protecting some legitimate Southern heritage, or the fact that the market does indeed create jobs and progress, or that wars do often liberate some group. That is the reason most of us cannot see the demonic evil. "Keeping our borders secure" is a worthy goal, but until someone names precisely what such a statement entails, it hangs invisibly in the air—to be misused by both sides in the argument.

As Paul notes, "The angels of darkness must disguise themselves as angels of light" (2 Corinthians 11:14). Evil flourishes in such a context, each side thinking it alone has the full light, when in fact both only have a partial light. Is there no middle ground between maintaining legitimate national borders and building a wall? There is that dualistic

64

thinking again, creating false alternatives and righteously choosing sides. Most cannot see this. Thus, Jesus calls the devil "the father of lies" (John 8:44).

It is important to emphasize that such evil is not first lodged in the individual soldier, guard, banker, pharmacist, or politician, who, in terms of his or her private morality, might be quite good and virtuous—and usually is. But, without knowing it, he or she is also a victim. Each must recognize that *they are a part of something that is, of itself, a beast when left to operate according to its own devices—and unaccountable to any norms beyond self-interest,* which today is largely the profit motive.

This is not to say that these institutions do not do much good, too! The evil lies in their demand for total allegiance, no criticism, and unquestioning loyalty. Remember the eleventh commandment of President Ronald Reagan (1911–2004): "Thou shalt not speak evil of another Republican"?[16] Without saying it, all sacralized systems require that we conform to edicts like absolute loyalty, patriotism, obedience, and proper protocols.

Why has Jesus' teaching "Do not take oaths at all" (Matthew 5:34–35) been considered unimportant, even though it appears in his first sermon? The oaths of which he speaks are often hidden behind phrases like, "the will of God," "the church says," and when we judge any non-conformity as being akin to sin. Blasphemy is the religious word, while treason is the secular word for the same thing. Idolatry was first considered the only and foundational sin in Judaism—to make something God that is not God and worship it unquestioningly. This is exactly what the first commandment prohibits (Exodus 20:3; Deuteronomy 5:7). Most people I know worship several things more than God, even good things like family or church.

In summary, I believe Paul and his school teach that sin shows itself as social, cultural, or historical *entrapment, cultural blindness,* or *bondage,* along with personal complicity with such delusions. Such bondage is in great part what we now understand as addiction, denial, and preoccupations that often become enthrallment, which the ancients would have called being possessed by a demon. This strange word "enthrallment" well describes humans when we are no longer in control but, instead, *under* control. When we do not experience any detachment from our inner wild self or enjoy emotional calmness, we are truly *possessed* by that mind and those emotions.

I do not think this needs much proof as we observe our present society, our culture wars, and typical political debates. Crowds seem ready to applaud delusional nonsense. They are truly trapped inside of a collective "demon" and unable to even recognize obvious truth or blatant lies. Think of American political parties that condemn a fault in the other party, but have no problem with their own party when it does the exact same thing. We do not really love truth; we love winning.

Winning is revealing itself as the American idol, at almost every level.

I remember asking my theology professor, back in the late 1960s, if we had to believe in a literal, personalized devil. His answer was fully correct as I look back on it. He said something to this effect: All the religions of the world would not have spoken so readily of evil spirits or demons if they were not pointing to something very real and universal. Maybe they are pointing to what we now mean by a constellation of energy, a "complex," or a force field of negative energy that feels tangible. Jungians insist that to personify something, as we do with the devil, is to give it an identity and personality. It is saying, "Take me seriously!" or "This is something with which I need to engage and not just dismiss."

When we imagine the caricature of a red, horned figure, we are not taking evil seriously. It is almost a cartoon, but it does give evil visibility and voice. Any image of a devil personifies the whole notion of possession: a state in which we no longer have much freedom to see, to find our own agency, or to love. There is indeed a devil at the door of the pornography shop, as so many Hindus and Buddhists dare to portray at the doorways of even sacred temples, warning visitors against the demons they are bringing into sacred space—and the demons that might already be hiding there. The message was clear in the many gargoyles on Catholic medieval cathedrals.

When we find ourselves so immersed inside a group-think and trapped by tears whenever the "Star-Spangled Banner" is sung (as opposed to "Holy God, We Praise Thy Name"), it's time to examine the nature of this kind of enthrallment; it is what some call "false transcendence" or ego enmeshment. In this sense, devils and possession by devils are, in fact, quite common. The ancients were not as naïve as we might once have thought.

A WAY OUT AND THROUGH

"For freedom Christ has set us free," Paul wrote in Galatians 5:1. Yet, few of us were taught that religion was a path toward *deeper and deeper inner freedom* (which largely shows itself as a more and more expansive freedom to love). Instead, most of us thought of religion as a private regimen of duty, social obligations, and commandments, usually about external behavior.

We did not learn how to see evil in its many shapes until the modern sciences of criminology, social psychology, the study of history, and human development theories helped us understand that *the causes of human evildoing are multilayered, partly denied, and not always immediately obvious.* I learned this personally in my fourteen years as a jail chaplain in New Mexico. There was the story about a wrongdoer that I read in the newspaper, and then there was the complex person I got to know alone in the cell. Only then was I ever capable of compassion, sometimes understanding, and often even full forgiveness.

Jesus was absolutely honest when he said, "Father, forgive them, they do not know what they are doing" (Luke 23:34). Most people live a largely unconscious life. *Most evil is first done more out of blindness and ignorance than out of malice.* Both priests and politicians mislead us when they point only to the most obvious level of sin or evil, pretending they have rightly named and exorcised the demon. Voters in the US who focus on a single issue, such as abortion or the economy, often ignore other major and related problems like poverty, racism, misogyny, the gun culture, and our *de facto* welfare for the rich, which then are allowed to flourish and go unrecognized

72

and unquestioned. Our attention is diverted from the social and structural sins that we do not want to see, or that the powers-that-be do not want us to see.

We cannot dislodge the plank upon which we stand. It is too often paying our bills, making us feel secure or moral, and giving us status. It is amazing how well this works and how few people can see through it all. (Is this seeing what we mean by wisdom?) Think of capitalism itself, which, in the US, disallows any critique or regulation. We leave it totally unquestioned and unregulated just because it is *not* communism or socialism. Meanwhile, the rich just keep getting richer and the poor getting poorer as income inequality widens at an ever-increasing rate. Is this really the best we can do?

Christians are generally not much different from everyone else in this regard. We are no more skilled at seeing the true nature of evil or recognizing we are also subject to it—precisely because we have the illusion that we

73

have spotted and contained it by identifying *individual sinners.* We tried to control and condemn evil in individuals—"Lock them up"— but that contributed to another illusion: that we ourselves are above moral judgment and even on high moral ground, which is more the sin of pride than anything else. "I am pro-life because I voted against a pro-choice candidate," we say, ignoring the many other ways we do not foster or affirm the lives of other people and life in general.

We can only limit and contain evil by naming it fully and correctly. Many "pro-life" Catholics voted for two recent presidents because they were supposedly pro-life, but they never took a single actual political risk to oppose abortion. This perhaps illustrates the way in which having a narrow and self-righteous view of what constitutes good ("I am pro-life" or "I am anti-war") leads to tragic blind spots in which evil and death can still flourish. Often simple people, children, and dogs can "smell" evil, as it were, while lawyers,

74

doctors, and scholars who live in their heads can be totally possessed by it, profit from it, and consider it both normal and normative.

Keep in mind, too, that we cannot ever destroy evil by a direct, frontal attack. It will invariably win by getting us to play its own game. Hand-to-hand combat pulls us into making the same strategic moves from the other side—in mind, body, and soul. We mirror our adversary without knowing it. This is the basic insight of nonviolence training, which itself did not begin to happen in most societies until the middle of the twentieth century. Nonviolent practices of responding to oppression and evil taught us—among many other things—that those who shame others are usually less capable of love than the sinners they shame.

Shamers cast their own fears and failings onto others and attack those they seek to marginalize. Doing so normally creates enclaves of limited and loud moral one-upmanship— often focused on nonessential issues. But each side plants its flag firmly in one of two opposing moral certitudes, and the battle continues unabated, as we see in the decades-old pro-life and pro-choice battles around abortion, with neither side willing to move their flag. Much of America's Congress is the same. Both illustrate how *not* to grow up as a human being. The pro-life movement is often just pro-birth and the pro-choice movement is often just spiritually lazy.

We need real wisdom and spiritual intelligence in attacking evil, or it rebounds back to us. This is probably what Jesus meant when he told the disciples that a certain kind of demon could "only be driven out by prayer and fasting" (Mark 9:29), which I would interpret as seeking both our inner depth and detachment from the egoic self. His response (Mark 9:17–27) was a correction to the *transactional* ritual exorcism ("get out that crucifix and find an ordained exorcist"), which the disciples were trying, instead of the *transformational* methods that Jesus always followed (real prayer for and with the person, and

76

detachment from our own agenda). It is the difference between a new student and a master teacher. Many of us say the real seminary begins after someone leaves the seminary and begins actual ministry.

Finally, as partially addressed earlier, because evil is corporate before it is individual, *it can only be substantially overcome by corporate good.* The lone individual is rather helpless against evil and also rather inept at persisting in good. Merely converting individuals to Jesus has never added up to changing culture, society, or nation states. In fact, the people in the US who seem most *incapable* of critiquing American culture are precisely the many individuals who have "made a personal [that is, private] decision for Jesus as their Lord and Savior" but have no sympathy for anyone outside that limited group and little accountability for what that decision means. Their goodness is too small, and the private self and its "salvation" is still the only real reference point.

Note also how most mass murderers and terrorists are invariably individualistic loners. They think they have spotted and confined evil in one place, race, or religion, and take it upon themselves to do the heroic job of eliminating it. They are hardly ever members of communities, neighborhood associations, or families in any real sense.

THE SPIRAL OF VIOLENCE

We must nip evil in its first hidden forms or it will always take over unchallenged in the private individual or the sanctified group. This is exactly what Brazilian bishop Dom Hélder Câmara (1909–1999) said many years ago when he talked about the "spiral of violence," in which institutional violence provokes a violent response, which in turn is met with "necessary" repression, and then the same pattern repeats, each level growing more and more violent without really resolving the underlying problem (or evil).[17]

The spiral feeds upon itself. The individual zealot tries to rise above "the filthy, rotten system," as Dorothy Day called it,[18] by attempting solutions (such as legislation) that usually attack the symptoms. That attempt may make the individual and state feel moral, but it usually does not touch the underlying causes. (Think of acts like outlawing prostitution while never addressing the social causes of prostitution, or building a wall at the border instead of honestly asking why people come across to begin with.)

Frankly, addressing root causes takes much more work and spiritual intelligence, which transactional religion does not teach to its members. Câmara saw how many righteous cures were worse than the disease itself (for example, communism as a response to poverty, fascism as a desire for social order, Prohibition as a solution to alcohol abuse, or our inability to tackle the issue of immigration in any intelligent way). *Our "cures" never address the primal underlying violence that most people have already agreed not to see.*

This lack of recognition of *underlying causes of evil* is the source of much of the moral powerlessness of most Christian nations, institutions, and individuals. Conservatives in general concentrate on the individual level of sin, shame, fault, and guilt, and resent references to any other sources. They blame individuals and groups or concentrate on individual willpower—or the lack of it. Thus, they tend to like religion that also centers on personal behavior or what they call *righteousness.* (Ironically, the word is usually a mistranslation of the biblical word for justice!) For them, there is nothing like a good fire-and-brimstone sermon to make sinners feel appropriately guilty, afraid, ashamed, conformist, and obedient—to control the riff raff, which is "surely not me!"

As for the modern "liberals," they first began to recognize and attack evil at the structural level (that is, "the world") in the 1960s. It was a major and tumultuous breakthrough in history and consciousness, but there were few available social tools or teachers who could fully understand what they were saying. They

81

attacked the world and sometimes the devil, but usually ignored the ignorance or selfishness of the individual. These liberals often ended up looking quite naïve and inexperienced, yet they still awakened the beginnings of the civil rights movement, the anti-war movement, and the War on Poverty, which would have been unthinkable just a decade before. Yet, today's progressive is almost in denial about personal fault, responsibility, duty, necessary guilt, or any notion of sin whatsoever. This is contrary to almost the entire history of morality. They end up with very sloppy thinking that the conservatives can rightly dismiss.

The only way out and through—for either side of any dualism—is a kind of *universal forgiveness*, the permanently bonding glue of grace, which seals in all the gaps that law and religion can never finally or fully fill. Paul's word for that constant filling of the gaps from God's side is, of course, grace, and sometimes mercy. God radically okays the imperfection of every human response and situation, and continues to work with it over the long haul. But that can only be seen with an evolutionary notion of religion, as we see in the work of Michael Dowd,[19] and a non-mythological understanding of The Second Coming of Christ.[20]

Paul's archetypal corporate image for entrapped humanity is Adam, who eats of "the tree of good and evil" despite being told it would be fatal (Genesis 2:17), and the archetypal corporate image for its resolution is Christ (Romans 5:12–19), "who reconciles all things in himself, everything in heaven and everything on earth" (Colossians 1:20).[21] You must admit, the mythic symbolism is magnificent.

In Paul's teaching about what he calls "the sin system" or "the law of sin and death" (Romans 8:2), the Gospel has freed us from this illusory system, even though we individually are still frail and weak. *By exposing the trap and illusion, he has undercut it forever, even though it will take millennia for this "mystery" to*

83

fully reveal itself. As far as Paul is concerned, the "law of sin," as he has described it, has been definitively exposed and death is destroyed. Just wait a while, because "God has done what the law, because of our immaturity, is unable to do" (Romans 8:3). Christ's crucifixion "under the law" (a murder legitimated by both religious and secular authorities) forever shows "the world how wrong it was about sin, about who was in the right, and about proper judgment" (John 16:8). This is a permanent critique of all of human history. Here, John too is convinced that this truth will only one day be fully apparent. The entire section of John 14–16 is presented as a giant courtroom scene in which the Holy Spirit is presented as the ongoing "defense attorney" (*para kletos*) who will slowly but surely win this case about sin and righteousness. Read these chapters several times, until all its levels of meaning begin to sink in. (If you prefer a football metaphor to a legal one, the Holy Spirit is always *running interference* for the soul.)

84

We are all on this journey together, and we are all in need of liberation (which might be a better word than salvation)—together. Note that God's intention is not guilt and shame for the individual (which actually disempowers), but *solidarity with and universal responsibility for the whole* (which creates adults). As Paul taught, "If one part is hurt, all the parts share in the pain. If one part is honored, all the parts share in the joy" (1 Corinthians 12:26). That is an act of radical solidarity that few Christians seem to enjoy.

In Colossians 1:24, Paul expresses this even more directly: "It makes me happy to suffer for you . . . to do what I can to make up all that still has to be undergone by Christ for the sake of his body." To begin to understand a passage like this, we all need significant rewiring of our extremely individualistic Western minds. I believe this desire to "help" God turns most of religion on its head. Ironically, I found it most fully expressed in three Jewish women mystics: Simone Weil,

Anne Frank, and Etty Hillesum. It is present in many Catholic mystics, too, but here it invariably got confused with reparation, atonement, and what often seemed like a masochistic understanding of suffering. I suspect we were just replicating our faulty and transactional understanding of Jesus' own atonement[22] and still understood justice as primarily retribution instead of restoration.

JESUS' CRITIQUE
OF THE SIN SYSTEM

Because he does not *directly* attack the religious and institutional sin systems of his time until his final action against the money changers in the temple, Jesus' primary social justice critique and action are a disappointment to most radicals and social activists. Jesus' social program, as far as I can see, is a *quiet refusal to participate in almost all external power structures or domination systems.* Once we have been told this, we will see it everywhere in the four Gospels. *His primary social action is a very simple lifestyle, which kept him from being constantly co-opted by those very structures,* which I am calling the sin system. We probably need to read that sentence three times at least. Here are a few examples.

The city of Sepphoris was the Roman regional capital of Galilee and the center for most money, jobs, and power in the region. It was also just nine miles from Jesus' hometown of Nazareth. Yet there is no record that Jesus ever went there, nor is it mentioned once in the New Testament, even though he and his dad were carpenters or "workmen" and he traveled through many other cities, much farther away. He also seems to have avoided the monetary system as much as possible by using "a common purse" (John 12:6, 13:29)— voluntary "communism," you might say!

Jesus critiques the doctors who made a poor woman spend all she had "while she only grew worse" (Mark 5:26). His three-year ministry is, in effect, offering *free healing and healthcare* for any who want it (Jew and non-Jew, worthy and unworthy). He consistently treats women with a dignity and equality that is almost unknown in an entirely patriarchal culture. He never marries, which could be interpreted as a critique of the idealized family

88

consisting of father, mother, and children (which became the justification for Catholic priests' celibacy and the vocation of single life). He clearly respects eunuchs, which would have been the generic term for alternative genders (see Matthew 19:12), probably inspired by the universalism of Isaiah 56:4–5. Then, at the end of his life, he surrenders to the punitive systems of both empire and religion by letting them judge, torture, and murder him. *He is finally a full victim of the systems that he refused to worship. Is this not a much more coherent explanation of why Jesus died?*

I could give many more examples of how Jesus largely ignored, subverted, and thus critiqued most major power systems of his time. Walter Wink wisely called them "domination systems."[23] Jesus knew the destructive power they usually wielded over the poor, the defenseless, and the outsider in every culture. When he does take on the temple system directly (Mark 11:15–18), he is killed within a week. Contrary to history's interpretation of Jesus' practice, *he did not concentrate on personal, "flesh" sins nearly as much as the sins of "the world" and "the devil,"* but few of us were taught to see him that way. The Establishments of the world like to keep our attention quite narrow and limited, and away from their shenanigans.

In fact, Jesus is always *forgiving individual sinners*, which was a problem for the righteous from the beginning (Luke 7:34, for example). In contrast, I do not once see him "forgiving" the sins of systems and empires. Instead, he just makes them show themselves (Mark 5:8) and name themselves (Mark 5:9)—just like Mahatma Gandhi (1869–1948) in India and Martin Luther King, Jr. (1929–1968) in America. When Jesus asked the demon-possessed man his name, he said it was "Legion," the term for a major Roman military unit. To the Jews, that word connoted only one thing— Roman military occupation and oppression. He treats it as a devil and sends it into the pigs.

90

I guess we would now call Jesus' whole approach "nonviolent resistance" (although the pig herders would not have agreed, nor the money changers in the temple, I suppose). He doesn't fight systems directly; he just refuses to support or engage them. He does use verbal violence against the religious leaders, calling them hypocrites or "whitewashed tombs" (Matthew 23:25, 27). Nonviolence is more than being "nice," it seems. Dualistic clarity about evil must precede our non-dual response or we end up with false moral equivalences, as we saw from the US president in his comments on the 2017 Charlottesville white supremacist march.

We resist in the same way whenever we refuse to buy from unjust corporations, when we stop using so much plastic, when we stand up for immigrants, or when we publicly protest an unjust law. (Catholic moral theology teaches that we only have to obey *just* laws, not unjust ones, yet I will regularly hear Catholic authority figures shout, "But it is against the law!" This is the sad result of poor catechesis.) Such responses do not have the heroics of a full, frontal attack on evil, but if we acted in real solidarity around such practices, think of the evil that would be eliminated, or at least mitigated, in this world. Even the seemingly impenetrable "walls of Jericho" might come tumbling down, as the Black community experienced with the civil rights movement in the 1960s (although we built those walls right back up).

Remember, corporate evil can only be overcome by corporate good, as Martin Luther King, Jr. did when he led his people to operate as one and in a nonviolent way. Think also of the choices the Amish and other such groups have made not to cooperate with the dominant system (not fighting wars, not driving cars, not wearing fancy clothes, not taking interest on loans, not owning televisions). I am not saying we all *must* do those very things all the time, but they are evidence of the potency of church community. How about doing these some of the time? Each of these is very much worth considering.

HOW TO SURVIVE,
AND EVEN THRIVE

Seeing the sources of evil in all their subtlety
and ubiquity led Paul to a very agonizing
problem and dilemma. If this is the nature of
sin and evil, what hope does any of us have?
Is there no exit? Is there anything we can do
to improve the human situation? The realization of this problem reaches its denoue-
ment in Paul's moment of near despair at
the end of one of his painful inner dialogues
(Romans 7:14–23): "What a wretched man I
am! Who will deliver me from this embodied
system of death?" (Romans 7:24, my translation). Evil is seemingly a field of invisible
energy from which he can never totally extri-
cate himself. There is no pedestal of purity

on which he can stand and rise judgmentally above humanity—which religion gave him the impression he could.

There is no high moral ground outside of sin, except the always *half-successful struggle itself* (Show me a totally successful reform or revolution!), which Jews to this day speak of as *tikkun olam*, the repairing of the world, which is always and forever in need of repair. This is different than fully changing the world, I'm sorry to say. The Gospel of the crucified and resurrected one is no idealistic philosophy, but radical Jewish and biblical realism. It is the task to which God in Jesus says yes, by becoming flesh (John 1:14) and emptying himself into the full human situation, "even death on the cross" (Philippians 2:7–8).

The Gospel message is utterly realistic about the world, the flesh, and the devil, revealing all of them, not just one of them. It teaches humans *how to spiritually survive and even thrive inside of a basic absurdity.* Most of

Jesus' and Paul's teachings offer a way to live inside of all domination systems by *identification and solidarity with those excluded from these systems, thus creating parallel or alternative communities.* The Gospel is not the straight line of the Western philosophy of progress, which wants to deny or reject— or completely change—the impossible situation.

This does not mean we should not or must not work for change! Instead, Jesus and Paul show us how to find freedom inside of the commonly unjust situation—and work for justice, fully knowing this is a much slower rate of change, but also a process which ensures spiritual growth, nonviolence, and some levels of peace. It does not lend itself to zealots or what we now call ideologues, which was surely the symbolism of both Simon the Zealot (who apparently grew) and Judas (who could not make the change). Integral Theory calls such zealots "Mean Greens," who have moved beyond the lower-level

97

violent ideologies, but are still quite arrogant and individualistic, not having inner God experience.[24]

Both Jesus and Paul radically reframe the human situation and invite us to live *a vulnerable human life in communal solidarity with both sin and salvation.*

• Neither of these could ever be exclusively *mine,* but both of them are collectively *ours!*

• Universal solidarity is the important lesson, not private salvation.

• We hold responsibility for all instead of blaming one or the other.

• *Human solidarity is the goal,* not moral superiority or perfection.

I know that does not, at first, feel like a strategy for successful living, and it is certainly not one that will ever appeal to the upwardly mobile or the pure idealists. It first feels like capitulation, but that is not Jesus' or

Paul's intention at all—quite the opposite. Paul believes he has found a new kind of victory and freedom. He himself calls it "folly" or "foolishness" (1 Corinthians 1:21, 25, 27; 4:10), as it is for most people to this day. He often calls it a "hidden mystery" that only the wise discover. (Most of 1 Corinthians 1 and 2 is called his *sermo sapientiae*, or sermon on wisdom, where he describes this alternative way of knowing that is different from mere philosophy or religion.)

Paul believes there is a hidden, cruciform shape to reality, even revealed in the geometry of the cross (see Ephesians 2:13–22). The world is filled with contradictions, false alternatives, zero-sum games, paradoxes, and unresolvable evils (almost all animals die a very painful death, one way or another; there have been four or five mass extinctions in geological time; children die young and evil people live to old age).

Paul is an utter realist about life on this planet. We must fully recognize and surrender to this foundational reality before we try to think we can repair the world with freedom and love (*tikkun olam*). For Paul, his insight is symbolized in the scandalous image of a man on the cross, the Crucified God who fully accepts and transforms this tragic human situation through love. If this is the reality to which even God must submit, then surely we must and can do the same. *It is not so much submitting to a new religion as submitting to an obvious reality, which is much more difficult indeed.*

By giving ourselves to this primary human absurdity, which shows itself in patience, love, and forgiveness toward all things (Christ is another name for every thing), we, in fact, find a positive and faith-filled way through "the world, the flesh, and the devil." This is not by really resolving it or thinking we can ever fully change it, but by recognizing that we are all complicit in this mixed moral universe. This is perhaps the proper humility that most Christians have lacked in their campaigns for social reform. This is "carrying the cross" with Jesus.

Through this primal surrender and trust, God can still use our own, now cruciformed, shape for healing and for immense good— and even victory. True healers are always wounded healers and not those who perfectly triumphed over all evil. Let's get rid of our common iconography of Michael heroically slaying the dragon and redis- cover the less common medieval portrayal (at least in Germany) of Martha calmly pet- ting and taming the dragon! Neither ideal- ism, rationalism, education, nor religious law will ever fully overcome the inherently flawed nature of this world. On the last day of history, there will still be sin and injustice. Yes, we must work like Martha to clean up our little piece of the world, but we cannot put all our hope in full success, or we will always be disappointed and then angry. Is this not America today—and most cultures, if not all?

In and through living with this tragic human situation, we are made like Jesus and, apparently, like God. When we recognize that (1) this is the universal situation and (2) we all suffer and still rejoice inside of it, and seemingly always will, it gives us a compassionate connection with everyone and everything else. *Think of Christianity as a giant act of solidarity with all of creation*, much more than a set of rules or practices, which only get us started. It is what Jesus meant with the first words of his Sermon on the Mount: "How happy are the poor in spirit" (Matthew 5:3). We can then distill these Gospel insights into the following main points:

- For Paul—and for Jesus—the Gospel is not a utopian vision, but a transformative strategy that includes us in the renewal of the world.
- Confusing Divine perfection with a human understanding of perfection is always a win-lose game that demands exclusion of the imperfect.

• Divine perfection is God's ability to include, forgive, and even make use of *all* imperfection.

• God's game is always win-win—at cost to Godself and to us—and it thrives on inclusivity.

• The Gospel says that we come to goodness by accepting and dealing with imperfection, not by seeking any private perfection or superiority (which only the ego wants). "When I am weak, I am strong," wrote Paul (2 Corinthians 12:10). I call it the integration of the negative, which C. G. Jung (1875–1961) always thought Christianity did not know how to do. I think it actually does, but few of us were told about it.

• Humans often end up doing evil by thinking they can and must eliminate all evil, instead of holding it, suffering it, and learning from it, as Jesus does on the cross. This ironically gives us the active compassion we need to work for social change. I am still not sure exactly how, but this is the foolishness of the cross, "through which the world is crucified to me, and I to the world" (Galatians 6:14). I finally think I might know what this enigmatic phrase must surely mean: My acceptance of a cruciform world mirrors my ability to accept a cruciform me. (I am *still* not sure which comes first.)

• God's plan of winning by losing is the "hidden mystery" (Ephesians 1:9; Colossians 1:26–27) and "hidden wisdom" of God since the beginning of the world (1 Corinthians 2:6–7). God hides so well behind the cross that only the humble and honest will find God.

• Atoms, stars, and planets have been surrendering to these asymmetrical forces of resistance, loss, and death since the Big Bang, thus creating the entire universe. (Chaos theory, dark matter, and black holes seem to comprise 95 percent of the universe. Explain that, rational thinkers.)

• Only humans resist and deny this universal pattern of loss and renewal.

104

♦ This is our real sin and our entrance into evil. We will only "know salvation by the forgiveness of all sin" (Luke 1:77), just as God does.

LOVE AND FORGIVENESS

Sin is not so much personal moral failure (although it is that too) as it is humans trying to validate themselves in a world where there is no completely solid place to stand and all our responses are flawed and partial. (I hate it too!) We can never be fully "saved" in this world; everything human disappoints on some level.

As many saints have said, *sinners are just grasping for Love in all the wrong places and in ways that will never work.* This has become more obvious to me the older I get, as I have had to admit the faults and failings of most of my heroes, myself, every religion and denomination, and every form of government. God has created a world where there is no technique or magical method for purity or perfection, but where forgiving love is the only way out and the only final answer: God's infinite Love and our ability to endlessly draw upon it. There is only the needing, the hoping, and the striving, and that is our victory in itself.

Here is the key to understanding this: Sin, evil, and disorder *included and forgiven* is the Divine Order! The absolute centrality of forgiveness in Jesus' teaching should make this obvious. Forgiveness does not nullify or eliminate the offensive action. It acknowledges and radically names and exposes that sin, evil, and fault did indeed happen—and then lets go of it! It does not, and cannot, undo it. It can't. Sin and evil happened. God does not undo the sins of humans or of history, but, from an infinite Source, forgives them. Every time God forgives—seventy times seven, apparently—God is showing a preference and capacity for *sustaining relationship over being right, distant, superior, and separate.* We are slow learners in that regard. The unilateral "covenant love" promised by the prophets is God's absolute ability to *sustain relationship with everything* and, finally, to overcome our resistance by the same allurement "that moves the sun and the other stars"[25] as Dante Alighieri (1265–1321) would put it. It is all one and the same stream of Love.

THE PAULINE DIALECTIC

To pull us into experiencing our absolute need for such love and mercy, Paul consistently teaches in a very dialectical way, by juxtaposing classic issues that pull us inside this unsolvable human dilemma. Paul offers the usual two elements of any composite and then jumps into a totally new composition. Juxtaposition allows him to draw essential ideas from two sources without fully accepting or rejecting either one. (It is only his distinction between flesh and spirit that he never clearly resolves by making the distinction too wide. In other cases, he largely does, but often in different letters.)

One could almost say Paul creates problems for us more than solving problems for us as a way of teaching us. He learned that from Jesus, who does exactly the same, especially in his parables. If we are honest, his method leaves us with no alternative except faith in an infinite Love. As Paul wrote, "Saying all of this, what can we add? With God on our side, who can be against us? . . . When God acquits, can anyone condemn? . . . Nothing can come between us and the love of God made visible in Christ Jesus our Lord" (Romans 8:31–39). However, most Christians have never been taught how to hold the contradictions of this cruciform shape of reality inside of an Infinite Love, so we almost always feel compelled to choose sides, hardening the tension and division instead of holding it.

Paul must have known intuitively that we need to differentiate and distinguish things before we can find the hidden wholeness between them (or, as I like to say, we must

112

first succeed at good dualistic thinking before we go to the non-dualistic, contemplative level for any kind of resolution). First, we use our good mind for critical analysis, and then we go to the non-dual contemplative level for our response (which will feel much more heart- and full-body-centered). To use a pressing contemporary example: Honor true femininity, respect true masculinity—and then it will be comparatively easy to override this seeming split with true sympathy and understanding for our LGBTQIA+ neigh-bors. Most people just stay with the split—all analysis and no synthesis.

Below are the major dialectical poles that Paul presents and desires to resolve, but Christianity usually has not. To keep this brief, I will not analyze each one here, but I encourage you to do your own Pauline studies:[26]

- Unity and Diversity (1 Corinthians 12 on the Body of Christ)

113

- "Jews" and "Gentiles" (1 Corinthians 1:23–25 and Galatians 2–3)
- Law and Freedom (much of both Romans and Galatians)
- Weakness and Strength (2 Corinthians 12:10–13:10)
- Foolishness and Wisdom (1 Corinthians 1:17–2:16)
- Flesh and Spirit (Galatians 5:16–26 and Romans 8:1–13, but overdrawn)
- Old Covenant and New Covenant (Romans 9–11)
- Adam and Christ (Romans 5:12–21)

Spiritual unity is not the denial of diversity, distinction, or difference, but the *naming and overcoming of them by love*—exactly as in "Father," "Son," and "Holy Spirit," which ideally keeps us from dualistic righteousness all along the path and allows us to see some level of truth on the other side. The doctrine of the Trinity preserves both diversity and unity in the entire universe. Humanity had better do the same, or we are in trouble. Up to now, we have not done very well with either diversity or unity!

I will offer you one way to do this in the next chapter.

HOLDING THE TENSIONS

The German philosopher Georg Wilhelm Friedrich Hegel (1770–1831) created a dialectical methodology that is well-known today as thesis-antithesis-synthesis. This process has been used helpfully in many contexts for centuries now as a way of holding conflicting ideas. Mix blue with red and we will surely get some form of purple. Both Hegel and Jung have been understood to teach a "balancing of opposites," where thesis and antithesis produce the synthesis.

However, thanks to Cynthia Bourgeault, who is a fellow faculty member in our Living School, I have been introduced to a deeper metaphysical principle that she (following the Armenian-born mystic philosopher G. I. Gurdjieff [1866–1949]) calls third-force thinking. With third-force thinking, it is not so much balancing, integrating, or even resolving the tension of opposites, as *holding it*— like a live wire—until it teaches us something new, bigger, and better. *But we pay the price for it, not others!* This is pivotal and central.[27]

Thus the emphasis on silence and not-knowing in all schools of contemplative wisdom. We ground that wire in and through ourselves. Slowly it lights us up from within— but it is also dangerous, because those unwilling to hold that live wire with us will almost always think of us as heretics, sinners, or just wrong and stupid. As Jesus rightly noted, "This is how they persecuted the prophets before you" (Matthew 5:12).

Let me offer you my very simple explanation of what we mean by third-force thinking, because I really believe this is what Paul is trying to do in his brilliant and subtle presentation of so many dualistic opposites. This method does not seek to make us choose and defend sides, which is what most of us do, but to move us to a higher, deeper, or broader level (whichever applies) for our response.

Think of it this way. First, every arising of a seemingly new idea or era is what Gurdjieff calls *Holy Affirming*. He uses the word "holy" to describe all three elements so we do not initially apply value judgments to them, but let the process play out. I think this is brilliant. Holy Affirming does not always have to be a positive arising, however. It could seem uncertain, ambiguous, or even negative (for example, the French and American Revolutions were good for some and disastrous for others, the Industrial Revolution was a mixed blessing, and on and on).

Next, each new arising will necessarily and eventually elicit pushback in some form, which is *Holy Denying*. The egalitarian French Revolution is quickly followed by the Emperor Napoleon. The high-minded American Declaration of Independence never addresses its indigenous peoples' rights, slavery, or women's right to vote—setting us up for the eventual, equally strong pushback. Critique is necessary for the refinement of anything and is thus also called "holy." Even the second law of thermodynamics states that every action will elicit an equal and opposite reaction. Jesus is addressing this directly when he commands his own tribal consciousness and culture to "love your enemies" (Matthew 5:43). *Resistance is necessary to the movement forward, even though none of us likes it. Resistance is not of itself evil,* except for people who make it their life's mission and become negative or hateful. We must somehow *love* all of reality, forgive it, allow it, and thus make it "holy." The more we can include and forgive, the more we transcend to mature levels of consciousness.

As we hold the very real tension of both Holy Affirming and Holy Denying, it should and often does call forth a higher level of consciousness which is *Holy Reconciling* (or *Holy Neutralizing*). I am convinced this is the core

120

meaning of our word "faith." (Picture the three Marys standing firmly at the foot of the cross, holding absurdity and tragedy together with hope.) But know that Holy Reconciling is an *independent force* and not the product of the other two; it is not a synthesis of thesis and antithesis. Instead, it is an X factor that Christians would call grace or Divine Providence and secularists would call luck, synchronicity, chance, or timing. All are true.

Gurdjieff insisted these three forces of affirming, denying, and reconciling were roles that need to be played for any movement forward; they were not persistently good or bad identities in themselves. Most recent Roman Catholic Popes said several very wise things and several very unwise things during their pontificates; the same with the Reformers. For which statements are you going to love or hate them?

The "good guy" and the "bad guy" might well change roles in the long-term movement forward. In fact, that is what we must allow, but which our controlling ego hates! This is why we must withhold initial and harsh judgments with each arising. *We never know for certain where we are in the process!* This is the best argument for non-judgment I can find. Only gentle and non-egoic critiques are allowed, as my kind editors do with unclear elements in my writing style!

But this is not the end. Each Holy Reconciling soon becomes a new Holy Affirming, and the process moves forward again, however slowly: awaiting, needing, and expecting new critical pushback and new resolution. We always eventually come to a new level in some way. That is evolution 101. It is also nonviolence training 201.

I believe it will take such third-force thinking to absorb a mature understanding of evil and sin.

• Holy Affirming might be assumptions about the way our system now operates (the current assumed *order*). For example, the naïve belief that white privilege does not exist in America, or exists but isn't harmful.

- Holy Denying is our ability to see through this homeostasis or status quo (the *disorder* necessary for change), as we saw in the nation's response to the Unite the Right protest asserting white privilege in Charlottesville, Virginia, in 2017.

- Holy Reconciling is the ability to transform and make use of both order and disorder, which allows a new consciousness to arise (a new, but always temporary, *reorder*). This would be something like, "My gosh, white privilege is still alive and well in America, so we need to quickly refine our notion of ourselves. We never recognized this before."

We must not confuse this third-force thinking with a simplistic or false moral equivalence between two sides. To simply say "there were good people on both sides" is actually to refuse to hold the tension. *We must first succeed at finding dualistic clarity between good and evil and then*

123

also wait and pray for a non-dual response—which usually does not completely please either side, but only other people of third-force consciousness. Contemplatives and saints will almost always be marginalized as ineffective—at least at first. "I send you out like lambs among wolves," Jesus says (Luke 10:3).

IN SUMMARY

In his writings on sin and evil, Paul appears to be declaring:

* Law is good, but a limited good; faith is better.
* Religion is good, but each religion is also a closed, imperfectly stated, and finite system; grace is better.
* Sin is evil, but sin is also defined and legitimated differently by each group; real sin is often well-hidden and must be located beyond the isolated individual.
* Virtue is good, but virtue is often well-disguised narcissism; real virtue is complex. "Only God is good," Jesus says (Mark 10:18).

- Reality is essentially tragic, but Jesus agrees to live within this tragedy, all the way through to resurrection (order + disorder = reorder).

- Therefore, this pattern of order, necessary disorder (exceptions to the rule), and a new order at a higher level (reorder) is the redemptive plan of God. Call it resurrection if you will.

No one completely "wins," or *needs* to win any longer, because, in God's great embrace, *all win when they can stay the course, even part of the way through! We don't have to win the entire race to still win the race in God's gracious economy.* This is the way that God alone wins and carries all of us along in one super wave of divine mercy. This is the Universal Christ, the Omega Point that lures history forward through an all-forgiving Love.

Hear anew the very last words of the Bible:

126

"The Spirit and the Bride say, 'Come,'
Let everyone who hears answer, 'Come,'
Let all who are thirsty, 'Come,'
All who want it may have the water of life
and have it for free!"

—Revelation 22:17

Only three requirements seem to be necessary to enter into the divine marriage: hearing, being thirsty, and accepting an utterly and wonderfully free gift.

NOTES

1 Richard Rohr, *The Universal Christ: How a Forgotten Reality Can Change Everything We See, Hope For, and Believe* (New York: Convergent, 2019).

2 For more on this topic, read Richard Rohr, *The Divine Dance: The Trinity and Your Transformation* (New Kensington, PA: Whitaker House, 2016).

3 Jean-Paul Sartre, *No Exit*, in *No Exit and Three Other Plays* (New York: Vintage International, 1989), 45.

4 Friedrich Nietzsche, *Also Sprach Zarathustra* (1883–1891).

5 Richard Rohr, *Immortal Diamond: The Search for Our True Self* (San Francisco: Jossey-Bass, 2013), 93.

6 Scott Peck, *People of the Lie* (New York: Simon & Schuster, 1983), 76–77.

7 Since I am praising Paul's genius, I must also point out his unfortunate use of the word "flesh" (*sarx*) in contradistinction to the word "spirit" (*pneuma*). Little did he know that later history would almost entirely equate the use of the word for flesh with sex, whereas his understanding was closer to our psychologically astute concept of ego (see Romans 8:5–17 and Galatians 5:16–26, where they are so clearly juxtaposed).

8 Ken Wilber, *The Religion of Tomorrow: A Vision for the Future of the Great Traditions— More Inclusive, More Comprehensive, More Complete* (Boston: Shambhala, 2017), 78.

9 Thomas of Celano, "Second Life of St. Francis," *St. Francis of Assisi: Omnibus of Sources*, ed. Marion Habig (Cincinnati: Franciscan Media, 2009), 481–482.

10 René Girard, *Deceit, Desire and the Novel: Self and Other in Literary Structure*, trans. Yvonne Freccero (Baltimore: Johns Hopkins University Press, 1966).

11 Ernest Becker, *The Denial of Death* (New York: Free Press, 1973), xiii.

12 *Even the Sun Will Die: An Interview with Eckhart Tolle* (Louisville, CO: Sounds True, 2002), CD.

13 This is clearly illustrated in the sins and gifts of the Enneagram. See Richard Rohr and Andreas Ebert, *The Enneagram: A Christian Perspective* (New York: Crossroad, 2008), 25–28.

14 Robert Bolt, *A Man for All Seasons: A Play in Two Acts* (New York: Vintage, 1990), 67, 69.

15 Anne Wilson Schaef, *Women's Reality: An Emerging Female System in a White Male Society* (New York: HarperCollins, 1992), 8.

16 Attributed by Reagan to Gaylord Parkinson. See H. W. Brands, "The Real Story of Reagan's 11th Commandment," *Politico*, April 5, 2017, https://www.politico.com/magazine/story/2017/04/11th-commandment-gop-republican-reagan-trump-214982.

17 Hélder Câmara, *Spiral of Violence* (London: Sheed and Ward, 1971).

18 Dorothy Day, "Money and the Middle-Class Christian," *National Catholic Reporter*, February 18, 1970, as quoted in Brian Terrell, "Dorothy Day's 'filthy, rotten system' likely wasn't hers at all," *National Catholic Reporter*, April 16, 2012, https://www.ncronline.org/news/people /dorothy-days-filthy-rotten-system-likely -wasnt-hers-all.

19 See Michael Dowd, *Thank God for Evolution: How the Marriage of Science and Religion Will Transform Your Life and Our World* (New York: Viking Penguin, 2008).

20 Rohr, *Universal Christ*, 20.

21 Ibid., 47–48.

22 Ibid., chapter 12.

23 Walter Wink, *Engaging the Powers: Discernment and Resistance in a World of Domination* (Minneapolis: Augsburg Fortress, 1992).

24 For more on this topic, read Paul R. Smith, *Integral Christianity: The Spirit's Call to Evolve* (St. Paul, MN: Paragon House, 2011).

25 Dante Alighieri, *The Divine Comedy*, Paradiso, Canto XXIII, 145.

26 Resources for such study include Richard Rohr, *Great Themes of Paul: Life as Participation* (Cincinnati: Franciscan Media, 2012), 11 CDs and Richard Rohr, *St. Paul: The Misunderstood Mystic* (Albuquerque, NM: Center for Action and Contemplation, 2014), CD.

27 Cynthia Bourgeault, *The Holy Trinity and the Law of Three: Discovering the Radical Truth at the Heart of Christianity* (Boston: Shambhala, 2013).